THE STORY BEHIND
MOTOR RACING

WRITTEN BY PAUL ROBINSON

CONTENTS

INTRODUCTION TO MOTOR RACING	4	FORMULA 1	12
NASCAR	6	HIGH-SPEED RACES	14
ON THE TRACK	8	RACING TEAMS	16
CARS AND DRIVERS	10	IN THE PITS	18

DISCLAIMER:
The activities in this book have been performed by people who are experienced professionals, or by people who have had professional training. Neither the publisher nor the author shall be liable for any bodily harm or damage to property whatsoever that may be caused or sustained as a result of conducting any of the activities featured in this book.

Words in **BOLD** can be found in the glossary.

DRAG RACING	20	RECORD BREAKERS	28
DRAGSTER CLASSES	22	GLOSSARY	30
DRAG CAR POWER	24	INDEX	31
CRASH!	26		

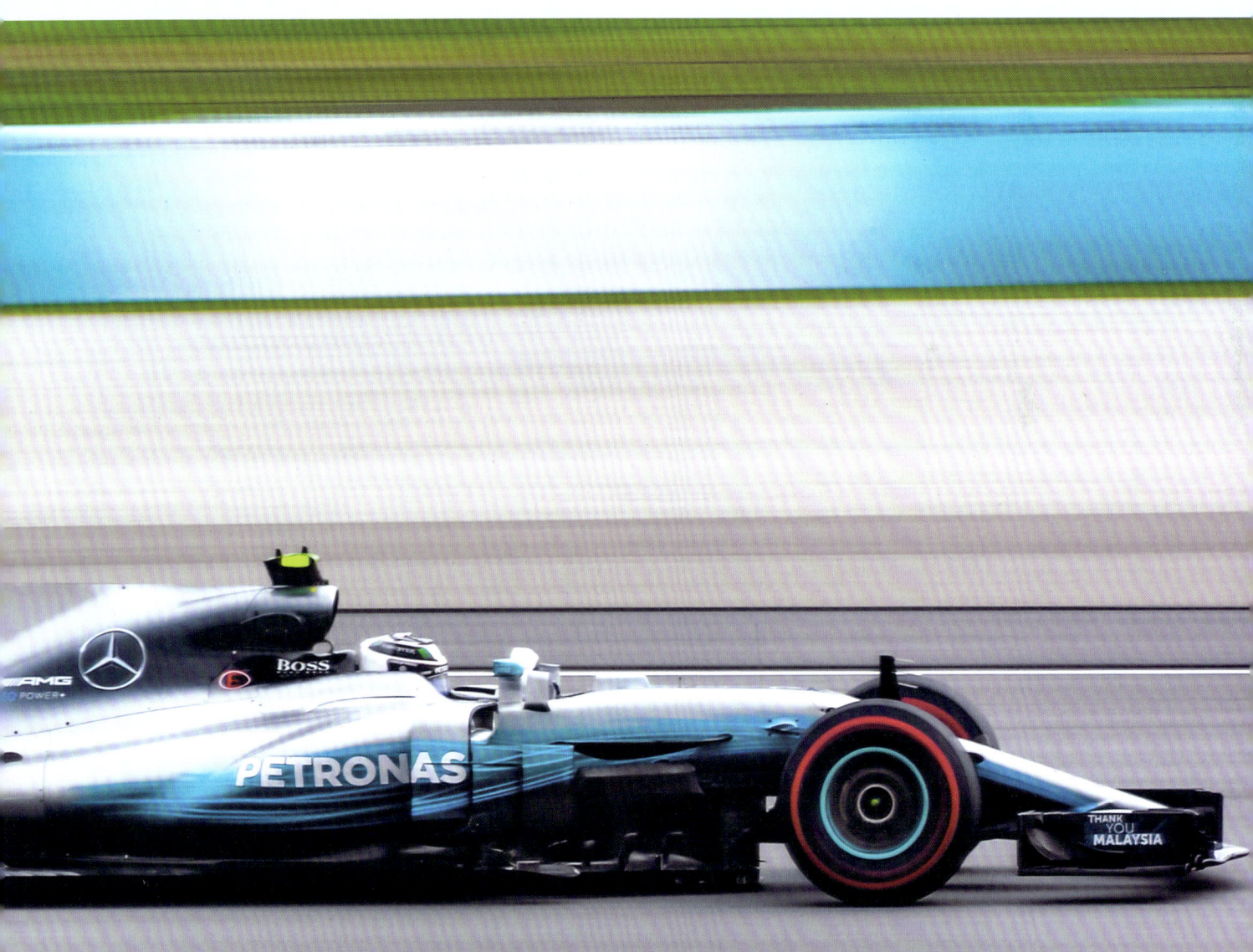

INTRODUCTION TO MOTOR RACING

All over the world, people are enthusiastic about motor racing, from amazing cars and their talented drivers to the high-speed races and incredible records.

ALL SHAPES AND SIZES

Some cars are built specially for racing. Others may look like the cars you can see on the street but they have been **modified** to make them faster. Some people even race old, beaten-up vehicles, or cars that look really wacky.

SUPERPOWERS

Winning races is all about speed! To reach top speeds, cars need powerful engines. Experts usually measure engine power in **torque**, which shows how quickly a vehicle can **accelerate**, and **horsepower**, which shows how quickly a vehicle moves during acceleration.

DID YOU KNOW?

In motor racing, acceleration is very important. Vehicles are often compared based on how quickly they reach 60 miles per hour (mph/97 km/h) from a standing start of 0 mph (0 km/h)!

TYPES OF MOTOR RACING

There are many different types of motor racing!

NASCAR

FORMULA 1

DRAG CAR RACING

BANGER RACING

NASCAR

NASCAR racing is one of the most popular sports to follow in the USA. The first NASCAR race was held in 1948, but there are now more than 1,500 NASCAR events a year, all over the world.

ALL IN THE DETAILS

NASCAR tracks can vary in length from just over half a mile (0.8 km) up to 4 miles (6.5 km) long. These can include purpose-built tracks and road circuits – normal roads that have been closed for a race. Up to 40 cars can race at once and races can cover many laps of a track!

DID YOU KNOW?

The first NASCAR race took place on a beach and road circuit in Daytona, USA! The biggest event today is the Daytona 500, held at the Daytona International Speedway track. This event kick-starts the racing season.

WINNING SPEED

Speed is key in all types of motor racing, including NASCAR. Cars can be pushed to reach speeds faster than 200 mph (322 km/h). That means when things go wrong, they can be disastrous! Crashes happen often, and some drivers have even sadly lost their lives.

SERIOUS SERIES

The NASCAR race season lasts from February to November each year. NASCAR has 4 main national racing series: the NASCAR Cup; the Xfinity; the Craftsman Truck (for pick-up trucks); and the ARCA Menards.

ON THE TRACK

There's a real buzz in the lead-up to the start of a race, as drivers prepare for their high-speed journey, and fans anticipate the excitement and nerves of watching the race unfold.

HOLDING SPEED

A **pace car** leads the racing cars on warm-up laps before the race. These increase in speed, allowing a flying start to the race. Top speeds are so fast that crashes and accidents happen often. This means that some cars don't even finish the first lap!

IN THE GROOVE

Speedway tracks are all **banked**. "High groove" racers stay at the top of the slope to keep a steady speed and avoid slower cars. "Low groove" drivers prefer to race a low line on the inside of the track.

DID YOU KNOW?

Cars often drive nose-to-tail, just a few centimetres (a few inches) apart. The second car rides in the **slipstream** of the car in front of it. This is called "drafting".

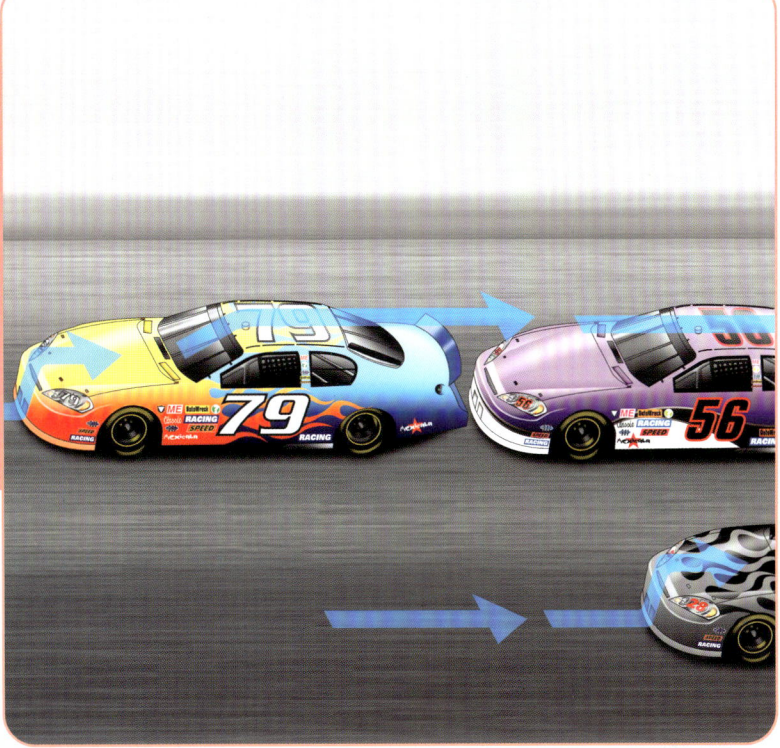

WHAT'S THE SCORE?

Drivers win points based on how close they were to winning a race, with the winner getting the biggest number of points – 180. There are also bonuses for things like leading the most laps in a race. The champion is the one who collects the most points over the racing series.

TRUE STORY

Dale Earnhardt was one of NASCAR's best drivers, with 76 race wins and 7 championship wins total. Sadly, Dale crashed and died during a race in 2001. His son, Dale Junior, is also a top driver.

CARS AND DRIVERS

When NASCAR racing began, competitors drove ordinary cars that had been specially modified for racing. Now, cars are specially built by experts for NASCAR races. Teams of engineers can make a NASCAR car in as little as a month.

SUPERPOWERED MACHINES

NASCAR cars are designed for speed. They are made of lightweight materials and have features, such as the front bumper, that force air round the car in a way that reduces **drag**. The cars are also low to the ground, which doesn't just make them **aerodynamic**, it allows them to turn corners much quicker.

SAFETY FIRST

Drivers wear special gear to help keep themselves safe in case of a crash. Racing rules state that drivers must wear a seatbelt, helmet – most wear one that completely covers their head and face – and a flame-retardant suit in case of fire. The driver's seat is designed to wrap around their body, and nets on the windows stop debris coming into the car.

TRUE STORY

One of the biggest car wrecks in a single race (in modern NASCAR history) totalled 31 cars! It happened in 2002 at Talladega.

FORMULA 1

The first Formula 1 (F1) World Championship race was at Silverstone Circuit in the UK in 1950. There are now around 24 races a year, held all over the world. An F1 race is called a "Grand Prix", which is French for "big prize".

TOP TRACKS

Grand Prix races usually cover 190 miles (300 km). Most races are done on purpose-built circuits, but some are done on streets that have been closed for the race. Because circuits vary in length, so can the number of laps that drivers have to complete.

DID YOU KNOW?

Most of the controls for F1 cars are on the steering wheel. Drivers find it quicker and safer to operate controls that are at their fingertips!

COST OF A CAR

F1 cars are extremely expensive to make. The main costs come from the design work and the engine, but individual parts like the steering wheel and driver's seat are also costly. Overall, an F1 car can cost up to £15.4 million (US $20 million)!

FEEL THE HEAT

F1 races usually last between an hour and a half and two hours. Being pushed hard for such a long time, F1 car engines can get incredibly hot. So can the drivers – heat inside the cars can hit 60°C (140°F) and drivers can sweat off up to 3 kg (7 lb) in a Grand Prix! They must drink through a plastic tube inside their helmet to stay hydrated.

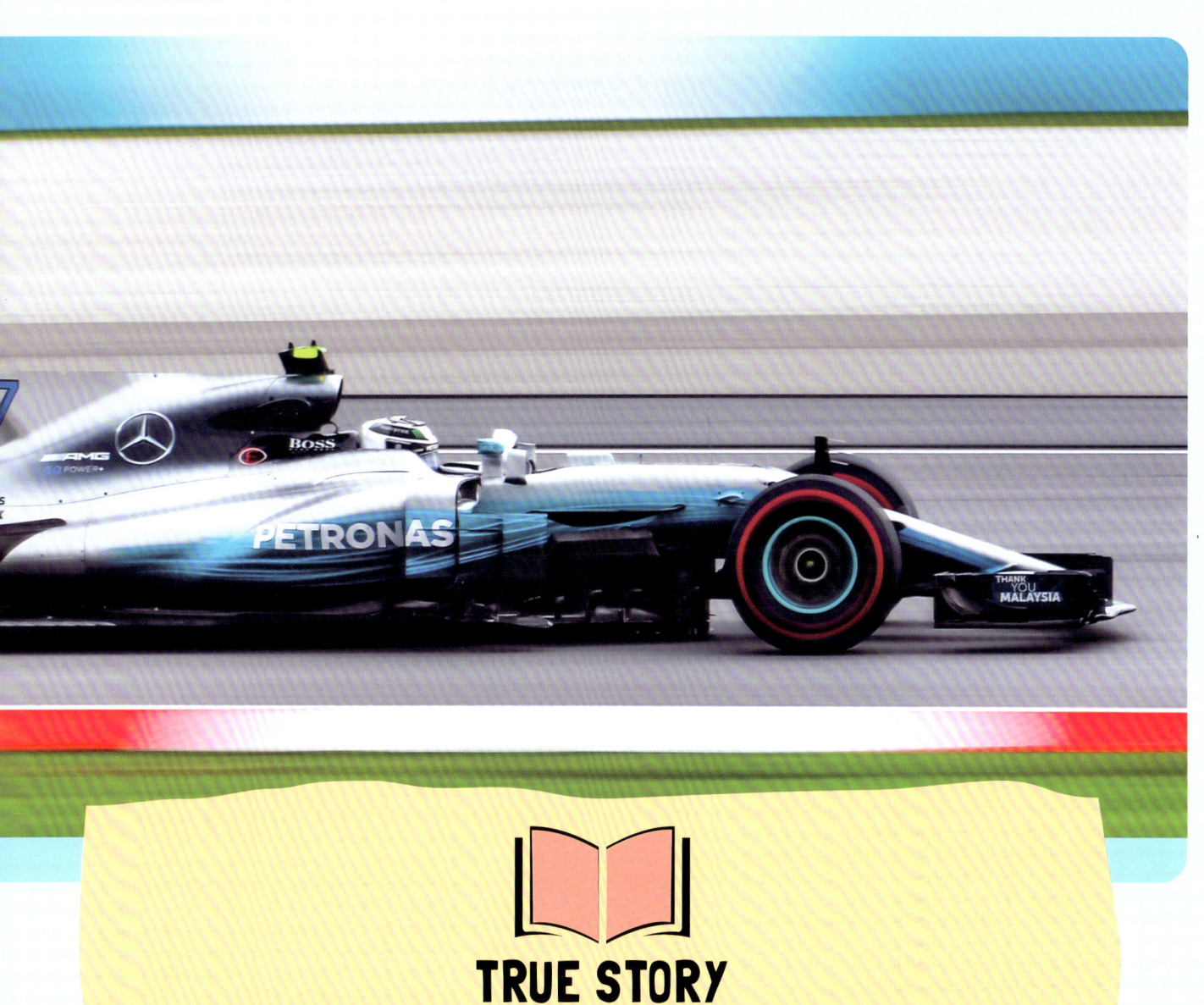

TRUE STORY

In the 1984 Texas Grand Prix, UK driver Nigel Mansell ran out of petrol near the end of the race. Nigel tried to push the car over the finish line to win points but collapsed in the 40°C (104°F) heat.

HIGH-SPEED RACES

F1 races are run in countries all over the world. Millions of fans travel from far and wide to watch Grand Prix races every year. The F1 is said to be the most watched international motorsport in the world!

STARTING GRID

Three qualifying sessions take place in the days leading up to a race. Drivers will try and gain the fastest lap to earn them pole position. This means they will start the race from the very front of the starting grid. On race day, drivers complete a warm-up lap to warm their brakes, tyres, and engines before the race starts.

TRUE STORY

At the Nürburgring Grand Prix in 1976, Niki Lauda's car crashed and burst into flames. Niki was seriously hurt with burns to his head and broken bones. Despite this, he was back racing six weeks later!

HOW TO WIN

Pole position is key because it gives the driver a clear start. Overtaking is difficult on most F1 tracks and crashes often occur in the rush to the first bend. The start is the most dangerous, but crucial, part of an F1 race. Pole position gives a head start to winning!

DID YOU KNOW?

Drivers sit in the "survival cell". This must meet strict regulations to protect the driver in a crash.

RACING TEAMS

Grand Prix drivers compete for their teams and themselves. Points are awarded based on where they finish in a race, with the winner receiving the most points. The driver or team with the most points at the end of the season becomes the world champion.

MAKING A TEAM

Grand Prix racing teams are **sponsored** by big companies, like motor manufacturers. Each team enters two cars in each race. Teams may have up to 5 different drivers. In 2024, 10 teams made up of 20 individual drivers took part in the F1 season, which totalled 24 races across 21 countries.

TOP TEAM RECORDS

Some people say Ferrari are the most successful team, because they've won 16 Constructor's Championship titles over the years. They've also had the most race victories, with more than 240 in total!

DID YOU KNOW?

Drivers sometimes change teams! Over his career, Italian F1 driver Andrea de Cesaris drove for 10 different teams! He participated in more than 200 races, but didn't win any.

STAYING ON TRACK

F1 works closely with the FIA – Fédération Internationale de l'Automobile – to host F1 events each year. The FIA watch over all motorsport competitions to ensure that races are fair and as safe as can be.

IN THE PITS

NASCAR and F1 drivers all have their own team of mechanics who work in an area by the track called "the pits". Race engineers use a radio to speak to the driver during a race. They monitor the car's performance, detect problems, and decide when to call the driver to the pits for maintenance.

A BIG DEAL

Pit crew members make sure the car is ready to pass inspections carried out by race officials. If the car doesn't pass the inspection, it won't be allowed to race!

NASCAR PITS

The crew chief leads the NASCAR pit crew. Pit crews must work quickly – they can make the difference between a driver winning or losing a race! It takes a top pit crew less than 15 seconds to **refuel** a car and change all four tyres.

DID YOU KNOW?
Many racing car engines have to be rebuilt after every race because the drivers push them so hard!

F1 PITS

While drivers can pit as often as they like, they keep stops to a minimum to avoid losing racing time. F1 mechanics need to change 4 tyres within 2 to 3 seconds! Since 2010, F1 cars aren't allowed to refuel during a race. They have to carry all the fuel they need for the whole race from the very beginning!

F1 cars are fitted with boxes that record information about crashes. They inform medical teams about how dangerous a crash was, and help mechanics and engineers improve car designs to increase safety.

DRAG RACING

Drag racing started on the dry lake beds of California in the 1930s. At first, dragsters were just street cars with parts of the body stripped away to make them go faster. They were nicknamed "Hot Rods". The first official races began in 1953.

WINNING A RACE

The goal of drag racing is to go as fast as possible over a short, straight course that's usually only 400 metres (a quarter of a mile) long. Two cars compete in each heat of a drag race. The winner of each heat goes into the next round. The last two cars left compete in the final.

TRUE STORY

In 1992, Kenny Bernstein became the first drag racer to drive faster than 300 mph (480 km/h), hitting an impressive 301.7 mph (486 km/h).

RUNNING THE WORLD

The National Hot Rod Association (NHRA) arranges most of the drag racing events in North America. They are held across 140 tracks. The International Hot Rod Association (IHRA) has different rules from the NHRA. Most IHRA races are on tracks just 200 metres (one-eighth of a mile) long.

DID YOU KNOW?

A drag racing car can accelerate from 0-300 mph (0-480 km/h) in less than four seconds – that's some serious power!

DRAGSTER CLASSES

More than 200 types of vehicles are used in drag racing. Professional and amateurs all take part. Young drivers aged 8-17 compete in Junior Dragster races. Street Car races give fans a chance to race their own street-legal cars on famous tracks.

TOP THREE

Professional drag racing has three main classes: Top Fuel Dragsters; Funny Cars; and Pro Stock.

TOP FUEL DRAGSTERS

These cars are the elite racers. They are long and thin, which helps them cut through the air at incredible speeds. They can cover 0-100 mph (0-160 km/h) in less than one second. In races, they can hit a top speed of 338 mph (544 km/h).

FUNNY CARS

With bright and bold bodies and big back wheels which make them look like they're tilting forward, these cars have earned their name! Rules around funny car engines are strict, but these cars can still hit 300 mph (480 km/h)!

PRO STOCK

The cars in this class look a bit like regular **production cars** – giving them the nickname "factory hot rods" – but there's one main difference. High-powered engines and fuel give them a top speed of more than 200 mph (320 km/h).

DRAG CAR POWER

All associations that set up drag car races have rules about how cars can be modified. The rules cover features such as the car's weight, engine, and body style. Most rules are there to keep the drivers, spectators, and mechanics safe.

FEEL THE POWER

Top Fuel dragsters have engines with over 8,000 horsepower – a number that is 40 times the power of a normal family car! They run on a high-power racing fuel, which has been used to fuel rockets. To add to the excitement of these fast races, the cars often shoot out flames of burning fuel behind them!

BURNOUT

Before a race, the car is driven to an area called the "Burnout Box". Here, water is added to the tyres, usually with a spray before the driver applies the brakes and spins the tyres to warm them up. It's called a burnout because the tyres smoke. The burnout helps the tyres grip the track better.

DID YOU KNOW?
During a max-speed run, Top Fuel racers experience an acceleration force of about **5Gs**, which pushes them back into their seat. In comparison, astronauts taking off to outer space usually experience 3Gs in force!

CRASH!

Most racing cars are kept in great condition, with perfect paintwork. But cars used in banger racing and demolition derby are old wrecks that are ready for the scrap heap. Both of these sports are great fun to watch if you like plenty of crashes!

BANGER SAFETY

Banger racing began in the UK. The cars crash into each other as they race around a track. The goal is to be the first over the finishing line – drivers do whatever it takes to stop their opponents from beating them!

DANGEROUS DERBY

Demolition derby is big in the USA. This is an event where cars don't race around a track – they smash into each other in an arena or field! The last car still running at the end is the winner. It's a test of tactics, driving skill, and car strength.

SAFETY FIRST

These sports have lots of safety rules. Like all motorsports, drivers must wear a seatbelt and helmet. All glass is removed from the cars, as well as **flammable** materials, like carpets and seat cushions. Many cars are also fitted with roll cages, which help protect the rider if the car flips!

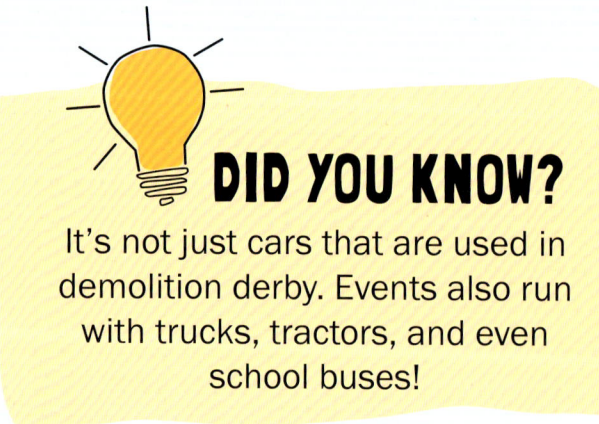

DID YOU KNOW?

It's not just cars that are used in demolition derby. Events also run with trucks, tractors, and even school buses!

RECORD BREAKERS

The history books of motor racing are filled with amazing record breakers. There's so many daring drivers to learn about. Here are just a few of the talented people who have done impressive things in motor racing.

MOST SUCCESSFUL F1 DRIVER

Many F1 fans say that Lewis Hamilton is the most successful F1 driver of all time because he's won the most races! He has a total of 105 victories (as of 2024!).

FUNNY CAR SPEED RECORD

In 2024, Bob Tasca III drove the fastest run in drag racing history when he hit an incredible 341.7 mph (550 km/h)!

MOST F1 WINS IN A ROW

Michael Schumacher holds the record for the most F1 championship wins in a row – he won five from 2000 to 2004.

BIGGEST WINNING MARGIN

Legendary NASCAR driver, Ned Jarrett, won an historic race 14 laps ahead of the second-place driver! The record was made in 1965, and no one has come close to beating it!

WHAT IT TAKES TO BE THE BEST

It takes lots of mental and physical strength, training time, and dedication to break a world record in motor racing. Depending on the type of record, people don't always break it on their first attempt. Once the record is broken, they also have to hold onto it! This means defending your record if someone else breaks it.

GLOSSARY

5Gs – a push or pull force that is five times the force of gravity.

Accelerate – to speed up. In racing, vehicles are recorded to see how quickly they accelerate from a complete standstill.

Aerodynamic – a shape that helps a car cut through air so that it goes faster.

Banked – a track that is sloped.

Drag – a force, like air resistance, that slows down the speed something can move through the air.

Flammable – something that catches fire and burns easily.

Horsepower – this number shows the maximum power direct from the vehicle's engine. It is sometimes written as "hp".

Modified – a car that has been changed and made more powerful.

NASCAR – a type of car racing. NASCAR stands for National Association of Stock Car Auto Racing.

Pace car – a fast, powerful car that leads a group of race cars when they need to remain below racing speed.

Production cars – cars that are produced in large quantities and made available for people to buy and drive on public roads.

Refuel – to fill a vehicle up with fuel when it's running out.

Slipstream – an area of reduced air pressure behind a fast-moving vehicle. Drivers sometimes like to tuck into the slipstream of another car to avoid the wind, and be able to travel faster while using less fuel.

Sponsored – when a company pays someone to advertise their company. In sports, a sportsperson or athlete may wear clothing or drive a vehicle with the sponsor company's logo on it.

Torque – the force with which something, like an engine, turns.

INDEX

A
Acceleration 4, 21, 25, 30

B
Banger racing 5, 26-27
Bernstein, Kenny 20

D
Daytona, USA 6
Daytona International Speedway 6
de Cesaris, Andrea 17
Demolition derby 16
Drag car racing 5, 20-21, 22-23, 24-25, 28

E
Engines 4, 12, 19, 23, 24
Earnhardt, Dale 9
Earnhardt, Dale Junior 9

F
Ferrari (team) 17
FIA (Fédération Internationale de l'Automobile) 17
Formula 1 (F1) 5, 12-13, 14-15, 16-17, 19, 28
Funny cars 22-23, 28

G
Gear 10, 13, 26
Grand Prix (see: *Formula 1*)

H
Hamilton, Lewis 28
Horsepower 4, 24, 30

I
International Hot Rod Association (IHRA) 21

J
Jarrett, Ned 28
Junior Dragster 22

L
Lauda, Niki 14

M
Mansell, Nigel 13

N
NASCAR 5, 6-7, 9, 10-11, 18, 28, 30
National Hot Rod Association (NHRA) 21

Nürburgring Grand Prix 14

P
Pit crew 18-19
Pro stock 22-23

R
Racing teams 16-17

S
Schumacher, Michael 28
Silverstone Circuit, UK 12
Street Car races 22-23

T
Talladega, USA 11
Tasca III, Bob 28
Top Fuel Dragsters 22, 24-25
True stories 9, 11, 13, 14, 20

W
World championships 9, 12, 17, 28
World records 4, 28-29

31

Copyright © 2025 Hungry Tomato Ltd

First published in 2025 by Hungry Tomato Ltd
F15, Old Bakery Studios, Blewetts Wharf,
Malpas Road, Truro, Cornwall,
TR1 1QH, UK.

No part of this publication may be reproduced, stored in a retrieval system, or transmitted in any form or by any means, electronic, mechanical, photocopying, recording, or otherwise, without prior written permission of the copyright owner.

A CIP catalogue record for this book is available from the British Library.

ISBN 9781835694282

Printed in China

Discover more at
www.hungrytomato.com

Picture Credits
(abbreviations: t = top; b = bottom; m = middle;
l = left; r = right; bg = background)

Wikipedia: By Martin Lee from London, UK - Andrea de Cesaris - Sauber C13 at the 1994 British Grand Prix, CC BY-SA 2.0 17tr. Shutterstock: Aaron of L.A. Photography 26tr, 27bg; Abdul Razak Latif 12-13bg; action sports 4tl, 8m; Adam Vilimek 17b; Bruce Alan Bennett 20-21b, 23t, 30br; Cineberg 19m; cristiano barni 5tr, 14-15bg; Dan74 15mr; Grindstone Media Group 6-7bg, 6bl, 10-11bg, 23b; Hafiz Johari 18m, 31b; Ilya_Levchenko 4mr; Martin Preston 5br; Michael Potts F1 16-17bg; Michael Stokes 21tl; Phillip Rubino 22b, 24-25bg; Steve Mann 5bl; Stuart Elflett 32b; Supamotionstock.com 28-28bg.

Every effort has been made to trace the copyright holders and we apologise in advance for any unintentional omissions. We would be pleased to insert the appropriate credit in any subsequent edition of this publication.